T0104745

AN ILLUMINATED DARKNESS

BY THE SAME AUTHOR

The Love Sheet
(with Barbara Fairhead, Hands-On Books, 2017)

AN ILLUMINATED DARKNESS

POEMS BY

JACQUES COETZEE

UHLANGA

2020

An Illuminated Darkness
© Jacques Coetzee, 2020, all rights reserved

First published in Durban, South Africa by uHlanga in 2020
UHLANGAPRESS.CO.ZA

Distributed outside South Africa by the African Books Collective
AFRICANBOOKSCOLLECTIVE.COM

This book has been printed in braille. Braille editions have been sponsored by Blind SA,
and donated to schools and libraries for print-disabled readers in South Africa.

This book is available as a free audiobook, at this link:
UHLANGAPRESS.CO.ZA/AN-ILLUMINATED-DARKNESS

ISBNS:
978-1-990968-66-2 (paperback); 978-1-990968-67-9 (braille)

Edited by Nick Mulgrew
Cover design and typesetting by Nick Mulgrew
Proofread by Jennifer Jacobs and Karina Szczurek

The body text of this book is set in Garamond Premier Pro 11PT on 15PT

Earlier versions of the following poems have been previously published: the intermezzo
(as "With My Father on the Lesotho Border") in *Absolute Africa!* (African Sun Press,
2018); "Difficult Poet", "The Days of 1999", "Cluttered Blues", "Mirrors", "Dian",
"Morning After", "Skin on Skin", and "Always Again" in *This Moment's Marrow*
(Ecca, Hogsback, 2017); and "Here", "Sorcery", "Funeral Blues", "Goodness and
Mercy", and "Table of Elements" in *Throw in Your Song* (Ecca, Hogsback, 2018).

For Barbara

CONTENTS

I

II

I

MOSTLY WATER

"We're mostly water, not solid at all."
That's what the travelling man said to me,
lifting his full glass absent-mindedly.

"If you want to stay true to what you are,
keep changing: fixed opinions are the devil's food."
I turned to answer him, but he had gone:

shifting shapes, no doubt, without a pause.
Stumbling outside, into a pouring rain,
I felt my bones dissolve, and I was home.

MIRRORS

I thought I could keep my mind steady
because I had escaped the despair of mirrors:
never having to confront
my own face, my share
of the incompleteness
of any solitary naked body.
What could be sweeter than such ignorance?
But everything I touch or listen to,
every line of every poem, every chord of the song
throws back some image of me:
private, visceral, and touched
by compassion, as if for someone else.

Today, on Kerouac's crooked road
across a vast continent,
I saw myself again at twenty-five;
not as I was then,
but as I wanted to be when I first read it:
one of the young men on the flatbed truck,
racing across state lines; a man
who could unhook himself from his own past,
from his fierce shadow at noon,
from the faces he sensed
in the mind's terrifying mirrors
that only he could see.

DUSK POEM

Then there were the two American tourists
(a man and his girl, I think they must have been)
who wanted to pray for me at dusk.
I pretended not to understand,
("Why me? Why not for someone else?")
but I was too obvious a candidate
to pass over in prayer, and they
emboldened by strange surroundings,
by their faith in miracles.

I sighed; I wanted none of it.
But they were sweet, insistent,
and my guide dog and I
had only just learned to walk to that restaurant.
It would be a diversion, after all.
I was hungry to slip beneath
the surface of this moment –
anything to be a citizen
here, in this private place.

And so I let the man pray
while the girl, soft-voiced and shy, deferred;
let them pray for the return of my sight
and immediately regretted it:
the young man's voice loud, authoritative,
desperate somehow, vulnerable.
I had done an improper thing,
willing them to believe themselves
into a corner, whether they knew it or not.

Walking away afterwards
I imagined them settling down for the night,
with desire perhaps unspoken, forbidden between them.
I thought of the cost of such refusals;
felt the old, familiar restlessness
that still sets me on my way through nights like these –
looking, looking past dawn for one more taste
of this incorrigible life,
so that one day I can say:

"I gave myself to this messy world
and tried to love it long after
I'd given up trying to change it.
No better than I should be, I didn't
stand apart. In the end
I redeemed myself: I wasn't a tourist."

THE GATEKEEPER

For years I used to daydream about it,
that short journey, head first
down the water-slide at Margate.

In my dreams that journey,
not more than half a minute,
was stretched over hours and hours, the slide

becoming always longer, the steps
I had to climb to reach its top
growing in number every day.

And each time, at the end of that fluid motion,
someone would offer me something:
sacred knowledge from a book, perhaps

or the love of a mysterious woman.
Always something extraordinary,
something meant for me alone.

Just the other day it came to me:
the gift I wanted didn't come at the end
of that journey, but at its beginning,

from the man who collected our money
at the swimming pool on Margate beach –
a toll-keeper of sorts. He must have seen

how much I loved that ride,
head first down the slide
and into the pool. He walked up

to my sisters and me;
said I could ride for free.

And I, self-conscious,
desperately afraid of the world's pity,
felt nothing then but annoyance at this man

who knew nothing about me. I was sure
he only saw my blindness
and not me, trapped inside it.

I remember scandalising my oldest sister
afterwards: "Ag, you should've told him
that I was retarded as well."

Generous toll-man, I can see you now,
collecting coins from entitled whites.
I'm sure I was not even unusual

in my thoughtlessness. I'm sure
none of us knew the luck we had then.
You must have seen a blind boy of eleven,

simply enjoying the ride,
simply comfortable for once
in his own body.

I never knew the first thing about you,
but I wanted to let you know
that boy's as much alive as you or I:

his unseeing eyes are already fixed
on some far-off goal. But for now
he is about to receive the blessing;

about to set out,
head over heels and in utter ignorance
on a ride he never earned

or paid for, given licence to play
by your unacknowledged grace.

THE STEPS

I

How many steps were there – fifteen?
I would walk up them fast, a book under my arm,
during each break, after every lunch
I ate at the school hostel, gritting my teeth
against the rude jokes; against anything
that could get between me and my book.

While the other boys learned to smoke
out of sight on the hard gravel, and the girls
did God-knows-what on the other side
of the world, I sat up there
with Paton and Cervantes for companions,
under the Little Karoo sun.

And all the time I was there
I knew only one thing: that I could see
through the bravado of the smokers, through
to the heart of things. I would read myself
out of that place, and into another, where hearts and ideas
are exchanged; where you can stand

in an illuminated darkness, having found
a place from which to speak; to write.

II

A decade passed over me, and there I was:
walking alone late at night, prowling the streets
of a university town, looking for an unnameable fix.
Sitting for years in my own safe house,
I had talked and thought myself into a trap of words –
others' words, old thoughts that had been thought
by others. I knew just enough then

to know I was a schoolboy again,
slowly descending the steps, finding my way
to the others, to the awkward gang –
smoking contraband, talking shit
like a human, revealing far too much –
saying things I would regret in the morning;
accepting the disgrace that must surely follow.

III

I still see them in my dreams sometimes,
those boys who went to school with me –
church deacons now, for all I know.
In the dreams one half of me's always forty-five,
the other half fifteen. Nothing is ever solved.

We know too little about each other, still,
for love or hatred. But
something always almost happens;
somewhere before waking,
something – call it hunger –

becomes familiar to us; is exchanged.

THE DAYS OF 1999

He would come home, already half-drunk in
the middle of a winter afternoon;
would sit down in front of his computer
and dream of poems, but never write a word.

He would feel the wine course through his body,
remember the ebb and flow of the talk
at the table where he'd sat; how he'd eased
himself into an altered state of being

to which, he thought, the words would surely come.
But no words ever did; only the hiss
of his blood in his ears, as of a sea
far away.

It is because of him that I still write:
because of his helplessness, the eager
plea of his young body, no longer mine;
for the words he longed for there,

behind the screen, the words of experience
he was too young to find;
because of nights like these, when I walk out
with a clear head, into these sober streets,

hoping still to find him.

SORCERY

I

The monk Milarepa, grown wise
in the ways of clinging and aversion,
forsook the crooked ways of men
in favour of solitude and equanimity.

Asked in old age
what he still desired from life,
he said: "In my youth I performed black deeds.
In middle age I practised innocence.

Now I am old, I want nothing.
To say more than this could only
lead to laughing and grief."

This morning, as always, I crouched at my desk,
sharpening my appetites,
listening for the beast that lives inside me.
Each day I scavenge for food and drink,
for the fleeting pleasures of blood and skin.

It is true that at dusk there is a moment
of pure emptiness, as if I stood outside myself –
listening, listening; as if I heard myself speak
in a dream, or from the other side
of a busy street. And still, I know

I'll set out tomorrow, trying once again to catch
the world in a net of words, to hold it
between my two open hands.
I will embark, once again, on the things
that inevitably lead to laughing and grief.

STILL AT WAR WITH THE STOICS

– for Pieter

I

It's not that I don't understand your admiration for them.
I have noted their dignified silence in the face of suffering;
have noted, also, the accuracy of their assessments:
how love remains an experiment, always on the alert,
always at risk of collapsing into mere biology;
how the beloved body is always breaking down at a rate
that is unpredictable, but steady and sure nevertheless.

I have read the dire predictions in all the mirrors that I cannot see.

And yet I remain mostly unimpressed by their dogged endurance,
by that blank-faced, solemn turn away from the body,
from pleasure and sorrow into virtue, into the heroism
of "I can't complain"; of "just getting on with it."
Instead I sit with the drama queens, with the hysterics,
the drunks; the ones who rage and rage, hoping that
even rage will become something precise one day, and almost noble.

II

Do you remember that time, sitting next to me by sheer chance on a plane, drinking unpaid-for whiskey; and me bursting into tears in the middle of reading my own poem aloud, to you, for God's sake? Such silliness, and yet we knew, we knew it was real – a poem, even if not first-rate, had found the place where love had been imprisoned and set it free, dispersing all that had been repressed back into the world again, transformed.

CLUTTERED BLUES

Cape Town bluesmen play too many notes.
We aren't meant to notice:
we are here as if in fancy dress,
murmuring beloved names –
Skip James, Son House, Blind Lemon Jefferson.

We love them for their poverty and rage,
the way their vision simplified the world
into black and white, and nothing in between.
We love them for their poverty, because
it happened long ago, out of our sight.

It has no sting for us, no reprimand.

I feel towards what it is we share,
how everyone tries to find a way back to that night
when Robert Johnson made his famous bargain,
and all of us almost believe
we would have enough love in us to do the same.

Later we will go home to sit behind our gates,
shut against the cold; with much clutter,
with the little love inside us that we will fan
and hope will grow larger. Meanwhile, there is no doubt
that there are too many notes in the solo

to which we are listening: so much skill –
but not enough space
for the earth to summon up its dead heroes;
not enough silence between the words
to hear the terrifying challenge

that would demand from us no less than everything.

RE-ENCHANTMENT

1

The first time it happened
it felt like the end of the world:
hot water failed to flow from the taps
in the old Stellenbosch flat,
when I was still immortal.

A plumber was summoned, the mystery solved:
an air bubble in the geyser; all that water –
an infinite supply it seemed in those days –
available, but somehow held at bay.
After he left we turned the tap on, and waited.

The splutter of water through piping then,
through interior worlds we only guessed at
for a moment, if we guessed at all;
until it flowed again: uninterrupted,
simply flowed into our hands, and we forgot.

Last night, reaching for me in the dark,
you asked me for a story, as you used to do
in the beginning. I felt the dry, dead air
in every cell, in every fibre that I could call my own;
language stopping dead at the gate of the mouth.

I held my breath, as if in faith;
tried to imagine those invisible pipes,
those labyrinths under the polished tiles
of an abandoned world.
And then it came: the first

stammerings of speech,
the flow of shared narrative between us,
weaving us together seamlessly.
I felt the slow enchantment taking hold
again, before my mind relaxed, relieved;

then drifted into sleep.

ON COMPOSITION, 1/2: TALKING TO AN ACTRESS IN CONSTANTIA MALL

The actress of Constantia Mall said she was keeping a low profile
now, after the many shows, the screenings;
said she had a small house by the sea where she could write.
I became curious then. "What do you write?" I asked.
"Ah, I'm a poet also."

She wanted to know where I'd been published.
"Do the magazines pay you at least?"
I said: "They publish you, and you buy the magazine.
It's a good deal, really. It keeps expenses down both ways."

In the silence afterwards she seemed to me
to be utterly appalled at such naivité.
"And is there a place," she asked, "where you can read aloud?"
"Yes," I said, "yes. A Touch of Madness
on a Monday night. You should come some time."

"Before you do that," she said,
"you should always put your poems in an envelope
and mail them to yourself.
I've had some of my best lines stolen, you know."

"Well," I tried, "they'd have to steal fast;
my poems are quite short as a general rule."
She put a cautioning hand on my shoulder;
said in a conspiratorial voice:
"Ah, but you see, they bring tape recorders."

ON COMPOSITION, 2/2: BILLY

"I think I know you," he said.
"I think I painted your house once."
He seemed far from sure, I thought,
but neither of us was embarrassed.
The evening had been softened for us already
by strong wine and half-finished thoughts.
Then, as the next glass was poured, he asked me
whether I had ever studied

the Egyptian Book of the Dead.
"They say that the heart is weighed
at the end of the journey," he said.
"It gets put on one side of a scale,
a feather on the other;
and if the heart is heavier than the feather
it gets torn out, here."
(He put his hand on my chest to demonstrate).

And we both thought, as we clinked glasses,
that they'd had the right idea, those ancient Egyptians,
not to hold on too tightly to anything.
I must have wondered vaguely about his heart,
he about mine. Thoughts half-finished, half-obscure.
I imagine he was up early on Monday,
painting someone's house, perhaps; someone
whose face would be easily forgotten.

As for me, I got up late in the afternoon,
my heart light and exultant,
knowing I had stolen all I needed
to write this poem.

DIFFICULT POET

Then there was the difficult poet
one Monday evening during open mic.
She said she had a lucky number, insisted
it should determine when she must read.
I'd spoken to her briefly in the bar
beforehand: a brief flash of recognition
at our shared love for the songs of Leonard Cohen.
But no lucky numbers were allowed
to influence the reading order
in such a democratic gathering.

And so she came on defiant, full of ire,
lines strident, awkward, grabbing
drunkenly at the world and
pushing it away at the same time,
until they steadfastly refused to fix
themselves in my seasick mind.
And then she sang – defiant, raging,
out of tune, out of step:
"Dance me to your beauty..."
She called me to join her song.

She called me twice, by name.

Ah, and I blush to confess it:
I did not sing with her that night,
nor on any other, even though
another's voice might have rescued her performance.
I wanted a song, sober and clear-headed enough
to look chaos in the face
without surrendering to it, while she
was too far gone to see anything
except a very private place
beyond all reason, language.

Difficult poet, forgive me for my sobriety:
such as I am these days, I need to keep my balance
to make the notes and words cohere and dance,
and you had slipped too deep under the surface
to remember the words of that song.

BLUE NOTES

Beautiful beyond words, these clear, blue notes –
these wild, blue notes that hang in the air
like a cathedral floating in the sky –
beyond the body's reach.

Music men, how do you make them,
these notes so pure and wild?
Listen, and I will tell you:
with your own bodies – muscle, blood and bone;

with your chests swelled out and your feet planted firm
and the song like a tree, rising up between them.
Its flesh and blood holds up this edifice,
straining against the pull of gravity.

DEEP LISTENING

It happened again yesterday:
in the middle of a fine conversation
about sublime and lofty things,
something inside me detached
and pulled softly at the pit of my stomach
as you stepped away for a moment
to pour wine for an honoured guest.

I could still hear the separate music
in our four voices, but the words,
the words had gone out of range.
The only detailed information then
came from the song of my blood –
subterranean, preverbal –
calling for your touch across the table.

There are no words for such music,
not in company, not when we're alone.
All I could say for certain then
to myself, under my breath,
was that all lofty things,
raised up in defiance of gravity –
all the immortal words, and all great music –

seemed to be reconfigured there;
rooted again in the fire
that sings and sings, unheard,
in our hidden blood.

HERE

Do you remember the one about the man who stopped
for directions and was told, You can't get there from here?

Comes a day like today when even the animals avoid you
and the songs fade out, embarrassed, when you turn your ear towards them.

Thinking's no good: thought is an insect circling something
for which your language has no word, pulled by a hand that was never yours.

Outside someone is singing for joy; someone is lifting dishevelled praises
through city smog; someone is dancing naked in the sun, knowing it will set.

Heart, you are too stubborn, too afraid to ask for directions. But if you did, if you phrased a question, if you had a voice on days like these, someone could answer

that even you might find a way to bliss; only you would have to start somewhere else: you cannot get there from here.

TO THE MEN WHO CHANGED THE ENDING
OF *KING LEAR*

It was not, after all, as simple
as changing the ending of the piece:
the good rewarded and the evil punished,
and sweet restoration of the status quo.

In the mind's uncharted darkness
the old man still totters across the stage;
beautiful people bristle with inexplicable malice,
and power is always hungry. That vision,

irrational and violent, how it knew you
by heart, dissected you as it dissects us still.
We stand amazed, and gaze and gaze
into the darkness of ourselves, which keeps its secrets, now as then.

Our questions must be barbed still, like the fool's;
our words, if any, must be clear and few.

and I remember the harsh cries
of the peacocks throughout that long day,
and everyone's shock
at so much unnecessary noise –
to what end we couldn't begin
to imagine.

II

LIST OF NUMBERS

I still keep their numbers in the file labelled "telephone list" on my
  slow computer:
one for the man who read back my half-formed poems to me in a
  monotonous voice, daring me to throw them away, until I slowly
  learned to sing more softly, urgently;
one for the man who fed me olives and whiskey though it must have
  been clear by then my being straight was not just a passing phase
  after all;
one for the woman who gave me a sheaf of corn because she didn't
  know how to say goodbye;
one for the woman who fed me rare plants and asked me politely,
  after I'd toasted her with the umpteenth song, if I didn't come with
  a pause button for God's sake;
one for the woman I hardly ever phoned, because I could not think
  of a question that would be worthy of a mind like hers;
one for the Greek restaurant that no longer exists, where I duelled
  with someone over halva and ice cream because we had no money
  to buy a second portion;
one for the man who dared me to do the wrong thing, to live
  dangerously, and then died of it;
one for the man who fathered me well, and then asked me, just
  before the end, to forgive him for his ignorance.

You can consign the body to the fire:
the bills, paid or unpaid; the outmoded
ways of being, and the very bad poems.
The names, the names are not consumed.

They refuse to be anything else than
the sum of my parts, hovering now on
an invisible screen, without ever
quite adding up.

TRANSPARENT THINGS

(after the diagnosis)

Today all things are
transparent – out of time; beyond language.
Even this face I have chosen
as I walk into your red room – I know
your eyes will see through
to the emptiness behind it.

Bereft of speech, I sit down
next to you; take both your hands.
We have entered a world where each word
must be weighed – calibrated, interrogated
for any signs of untruth; imprecision.

I would not dare to intrude here
armed with magical thinking. Already
we are being distilled, you and I,
refined until each fibre, each breath,
each slow, deliberate sentence
rings out, never to be repeated.

Come, take these hands; feel
their brittleness, now and to come:
this moment, this narrow
space, is all there is.

GOODNESS AND MERCY

I

You could say that it ended the way it always had to.
Remember how you would drop me at school,
only just in time for the bell –
stubborn boy that I was –
because I wanted to listen
right to the end of the song?
(Even now, this poem for you –
you know it will be dashed off
in the adrenalin-fuelled moments
before it's time to go, time to go...)
Only this time it was your body that ran
out of steam, out of rope, out of options.
(You can stack those metaphors any way you like,
and they still won't add up to the finality
of this first knowing, this first taste
of your absence from the world.)
The songs still play, of course, both yours and mine.
Last Sunday I found one of your old favourites,
one of those really safe ones from the fifties,
and it burned itself into a membrane
I never thought I had before:
good old Harry Belafonte
with his "Jamaica Farewell": "I'm sad to say
I'm on my way, won't be back for many a day."

And here's the thing: I'll take this grief,
take it with both hands; step over the narrow stream
into it, the way I couldn't trust my feet to step
into the warm, safe car in which you drove me
to and fro, to and fro, from school almost every day.
I will take it for the quaint, rickety rituals we found:
your "Goedheid en guns, goedheid en guns"
each time we clinked glasses, even though you knew
I was a heathen; though you had to stretch
the image of your god each day, so that he could offer me
the redemption that I did not, could not want.

I'll take it for that last fierce hug: me turning
on the stairs going down, turning one last time
to hold you in my arms on my way out,
because I could hear you thought
you'd said something wrong, out of place, at the end again.
There was no time to say it, but
I think we both knew we'd cheated that damned bell
one last time: two stubborn men
kicking and screaming their way
feet first into revelation,
into the goodness and mercy of the here and now.

THE GRIEVING

Sitting with my mother in the late morning,
having deposited my father's medical history.
This was all as he wanted it: his body,
even in its broken state, to be of use to someone.
Whatever we believe about the journey of the soul,
it's no match for this absence, this emptying moment.

Once, in hospital myself at the age of six or seven
(just before my first eye was removed, or maybe just after)
I made a deal with her: I would look after her one day
if only she would look after me now.
I am older now than the woman she was
when she heard me make that promise.

Twenty-five years had to go by,
and I for much of it in an unacknowledged rage
at the bars of a cage I couldn't see, before I would realise
that every song I'd learned by heart,
each poem I'd made, however desperate,
was an attempt to lift myself out of the grieving
that was always lying in wait for me.

Now we are adults I will make no desperate bargains,
and in return I will ask for none.
I know she remembers a time
when it was her job to kiss things better.
To nurse is heroic work, I know. I know.
But my work is to stay with the hurts
that cannot heal, the pain too heavy to lift

into speech, and to give it voice.
I will not dry these tears – not yet. Instead I sit
at the gate, allowing it to stand open for once,
and say, over and over, as if to make it true by force of will:
"We're not afraid of tears in this family.
In this family we grieve, and we are not afraid."

TABLE OF ELEMENTS

Today I suddenly remembered
the poster you gave me
for my university bedroom,
the one of the periodic table.

My girlfriend and I took it down
almost immediately: that list of elements
was more remote from me
than the words of ancient poets;

more distant than Keats' bright star.
I couldn't begin to understand
how you could have chosen such a thing
for the bedroom of your poet son.

   Today my beloved and I sit under the open sky
   on an almost empty beach.
   We've come to say goodbye; to celebrate you
   as you set out on your very last journey.

   We've brought a simple boat, made out of shell;
   a stick for a mast; a paper sail,
   emblazoned with your praise for the ocean,
   where your blood turned into foam for a moment.

There are clear shards of sound from the waves
as they advance and retreat; from the cries of gulls
that fly overhead, not caring about us
who have nothing to give them.

(There are shards of light also, but
I will say nothing about them.
A cellphone camera is recording
what may be shared of this moment afterwards.)

We wait for the waves to take your vessel,
and – I believe, for a moment – you with it.
We wait a long time before it happens,
so that I am ready when it does:

when first the sail goes, and then the mast,
and finally it is only the two of us sitting here,
acknowledging the space you occupied
when we could reach across and hold you.

I could sing you the song the waves sung to us,
sung as if to say that what we'd lost would always return.
I could speak of the circle of small shells around yours,
the opening that suggested we might learn to let go.

I could speak of the tiny fire we lit there
and the way my body leaned into it
as I thanked you for letting me go my own way,
just as I let you go yours now, belatedly.

But what I might as well say
is that I see the point now
of that lost poster with its periodic table.
Words being so brittle now,

it feels good just to enumerate
the elements that surround us here:
the rock on which we sat;
the approaching waves of the sea; the air

that was suddenly so empty
when the waves took you; the fire we made
for clarity; that burned so brightly in you,
that still burns in me today.

IN THE DARK ROOM

A man in the middle of his life,
alone with a woman in a dark room.
It is late: in their blood they can feel
the pull of gravity, of tired rivers clogged by sand.

What is it then that suddenly parts the air
around him, so that his clenched fingers
relax and spread in a gesture
that makes him almost beautiful?

What is it that reminds him of an old song
he hasn't thought of for many months,
until he starts to hum a line or two
absent-mindedly, from the middle of it?

He turns to her then, lies down carefully
beside her; tries to imagine what she might see of him:
a man in the midst of life again,
feeling it flow clear and strong through his open hands.

MORNING AFTER

Half past five in the morning: he comes awake
slowly; turns over on his back, floating up from sleep.

A long and lovely shudder runs through his body:
were they really together like that again, last night?

Then, between relief and bafflement,
he reaches his hands down the whole length of him,

of a body he knows he must learn to love again
as his. Then, only then, his left hand very slowly reaches across,

and gently (so as not to wake her)
finds her there, in the bed next to him.

APOLOGY FOR A MOOD SWING

Forgive me that I shook the bathroom sliding-door, till it loosened itself
from its hinges. I was remembering the fierce wind I felt
in the house the day before, when no wind stirred at all
in the quiet air around us. I believed
it wanted to suck me into the void
that must be waiting for all of us,
and in my rage I wanted to meet it
standing up, guns blazing.

Forgive me that I stayed out till five in the morning, and drank down
the second bottle of red wine without letting you know my whereabouts.
I had quarrelled with myself all that day,
and our love-bed seemed too sacred a place
for me to hide myself in.

Forgive me that sometimes I waste precious moments
before retracing my steps and finding you
where you stand in the emptying wind.
Sometimes my feet cannot remember
how they could have had the courage to walk with you
into such fierce, shared communion
over and over
until they came, at last, into their strength.

FUNERAL BLUES

– for Jaco Botha, 1972–2016

I know how I will hold you
when I can finally hold you
in peace, in a mind that is balanced,
as yours could not be:

ah, that narrow gaze of yours,
simplifying the world
to a white-hot flame, to a point
as sharp as a knife-edge.

It is the hunger I will remember:
the terrible urgency you brought
to your loving, so that women reported
on you as if there was a war on, always.

An hour before your funeral,
before the salesmen came with their sermons,
I ordered a beer in an art gallery
and drank to your health, though I knew you were dead.

I knew no sermon could console me,
not on this day, nor on any other.
And then I heard, over the gallery's speakers,
as if in answer to a question,

an old jazz standard, almost out of earshot;
someone ordering the one dish that would not,
could not possibly be on the menu;
for which no payment could ever be demanded.

You would have smiled if you were in my shoes then,
recognising that demand as your own:
"I want the frim fram sauce with the os 'n fay,
with shifafa on the side."

POEM FOR GRIFFIN

In your hands now
you hold the key to all things visible,
new instruments of measurement and science.
What should we wish for you,
burdened as we are with knowledge
you must discard in favour of new things?

I wish that sometimes you will lapse,
will turn aside from this bright age
and all its instruments for measuring things –
that, listening deeper, you will hear
a stranger, startling music of old worlds
that sounds in your name:

lion and eagle, earth and heaven mixed
together, pictured drinking
from a sacred pool in Nineveh
all that we, and this bright age, forsook.
May all things indivisible and simple
be beautiful to you:

rustling of leaves; the faintest smell of stone;
the deep song of the sea, our first music.
May you smile to yourself, remembering
how far back time stretches, and we
such a small part of it. May you find this world
a mad, sad, glad place to live in

before you are done with it.

DIAN

I

It isn't funny, hearing that you're gone
early one morning in winter,
six months after the fact.

I had drifted away from you, afraid
you wouldn't recognise my voice on the phone,
afraid I wouldn't recognise you.

I thought you'd remind me of my future nightmares,
of my own old age coming towards me.
I didn't want to remember you like that:

the vagueness in the voice, the anxiety.
Now, six months late, I try to recapture
your voice, saying:

"I mean, now, really," the exclamation
accompanied by a throwing up of hands
at the world and its small-mindedness.

II

Do you remember how you paused
at the end of the poem
(you were reading aloud to me from Cavafy)
when he asked the body to remember
lips that had kissed it, other bodies
it had held close?

You repeated the first line at the end:
"Remember, body..."
as if you were planting it
in the mind's own landscape.
To hold on to memory
of desire, perhaps of love:

to forgive everything that must follow in their wake –
our forgetting, and that
of all the others.
Dian, I don't know
the cost of knowing what you knew then,
the solitude and dignity of standing so alone

on the precipice of yourself;
only that we must have nodded to each other
then, as the poem ended,
across the years between us, the knowledge
that I would sit like this one day
in a world without you in it.

III

In my mind I can still read this aloud to you,
and you pour another whiskey into my glass.
The years are nothing: what changes
is unimportant, after all. Friendship
is always the same, across generations
and the intricate directions of desire.
At the end of the poem we are still there:
a dead poet almost brought to life
in an adequate translation,
and the two of us translated also
to each other there, to our enlarged selves.

REHEARSAL

Reliable as the dawn,
this slow warmth of the body:
each time our hands linger
on stone, over each other's
aroused skin, there is this
unstoppable enchantment:
the slow warmth that seeps from the body
and into the bone, the muscle of the beloved.

And this poem, as you know,
can only ever be
a rehearsal for that moment
when skin and bone speak
with an eloquence beyond our finest words,
and three thousand years of metaphysics
dissolve into the breathless dark
where two become one.

INLAND

Only the other day you told me how oysters
begin to respond to the moon,
to open and close even inland,
even in the desert,
as if they are still in touch with the tides of the sea.

We too are inland here, my dearest:
I notice how much longing
these words have to carry now,
though they translate into sound that still travels between us.

As for the moon? It is an unseen brightness
I love from the distance of poems,
like the one in which you described my features
sculpted by its light, as if in marble,
though all I wanted was

to pull you close, so close
that there could be no distance any more
between us and the pull
of that invisible tide.

WHAT IS REAL

What is real is the imprint of your voice
on the ground of my memory,
the way it entwined itself with the swish
of thorn-twigs against the truck
yesterday afternoon, driving to the game lodge,
and with the faint animal smell outside.

What is real is telling you that I love you
long-distance, and hearing it
played back like an echo seconds later,
and the lurch my stomach gives then because it is still true.

What is real is the distance
between me and the animals here,
the wire between us; the distance between
these words I read to you and what they cannot reach.

Nothing could ever be more real
than the way everything suggests your presence here:
overheard remarks and distant world events,
all weathers and the silence before storms,
and the lurch, as I say, my stomach gives
when we talk long-distance like this:

telling you that I love you, hearing
the old words echo back at me, still true.

ALWAYS AGAIN

You unlock the shutters, and the world
floods back into the room, as always. Then,
wanting even more world, we step out into it;
sit out of doors, under the autumn sky.

The first and last discipline, you say,
is to be empty enough to pay attention.
What do you hear now, right now,
in the silence the hadedas leave
in the wake of their beautiful, harsh calls?

Do you feel the coarse grain of the bread between your teeth?
Yes.
Do you hear the song of your own blood?
Yes.
Do you feel my mouth, warm, close to your mouth?
Yes.

I take the warm bread from your hands,
a portion of the bread of the whole world;
I imagine myself at the corners of your mouth now,
which I have kissed, and will kiss again.

A hinge, a shutter opens in me, then
I disappear into everything else.
This is where we lose ourselves; this
is the clearing where the world is made anew.
Only be still now. Nothing has happened yet.

PROPHECY

When those who are left standing,
or can afford time for reflection
try to understand how we lived
two hundred years from now,
and try to plumb the depths
of our utter folly,

will even one of them (tired perhaps
of mapping the inevitable
processes of history)
try to imagine how it felt
for two people to love one another
in such a world?

The relief of walking
into a cool house
on the hottest day of summer;
of turning our backs on the mall
and all the machines that were meant to console us
by making the world go faster.

And then to sit down and hold hands at the table,
in silence; until even
the familiar hum of the refrigerator
felt strange and loud, like something from another world.

And then the dusk would fall, and then the night –
perfect and sure and slow, as always;

and we would feel an inner space
open inside us, in a place
we used to call the mind –
but wild, uncharted, and lost to understanding.

And then, simply to sit there in the eloquent dark,
hearing the blood sing in our ears,
living this single gesture,
as useless and essential as a poem.

MANIFESTO

So many things I wanted, but to be
hollowed out, to be deepened by experience
until I sang more deeply, more clearly –

that, in the end, was what I wanted more:
the exultant, unpragmatic moment,
singing itself, saying "here."

This book is also available as a free audiobook at this link:

UHLANGAPRESS.CO.ZA/AN-ILLUMINATED-DARKNESS

―――――――――――

POETRY FOR THE PEOPLE

― RECENT RELEASES ―

Rumblin' by Sihle Ntuli

Malibongwe: Poems from the Struggle by ANC Women edited by Sono Molefe

Everything is a Deathly Flower by Maneo Mohale

Shark by Francine Simon

All and Everything: Scenes From A Winter Farmland by Kobus Moolman

All the Places by Musawenkosi Khanyile

AVAILABLE FROM GOOD BOOKSTORES IN SOUTH AFRICA & NAMIBIA
& FROM THE AFRICAN BOOKS COLLECTIVE ELSEWHERE

UHLANGAPRESS.CO.ZA